This Book Belongs To:

....

I am
Proud
OF
Myself

I
Deserve
to be
happy

I Can Make a Difference

I
Deserve
To Be
Loved

Today
I
Choose
To Be
Confident

I am
Free
To Make
My Own
Choices

Today I am a Leader

Today
I am
Grateful

I Forgive
Myself
For My
Mistakes

I am
Capable

My Life
Is
Beautiful

I am
I important

I can And I will

I am
Enough

Doing My
Best Is
Enough

I Can
Be
Anything
I want To
Be

I am a Good Person

Today Is The Perfect Day To Day Be Happy

Mistakes
Are
How
I
Grow

I Can Handle This

I
am
Valuable

There Is
Always a
Raison
To
Smile

I
Believe
in
Myself
And My
Abilities

I am
Open
And
Ready
To Learn

I
Have
Courage
And
Confidence

I
Believe
In my
goals
And
Dreams

I
Can
Do
Better
Next
Time

Everything Will Be Okay

I am capable of so much

Every Day
Is a
Fresh
Start

www.ingramcontent.com/pod-product-compliance
Lightning Source LLC
Chambersburg PA
CBHW081438250726
48662CB00009B/2844